D1413492

TOLSTOY IN 90 MINUTES

Tolstoy
IN 90 MINUTES

Paul Strathern

IVAN R. DEE
CHICAGO

TOLSTOY IN 90 MINUTES. Copyright © 2006 by Paul
Strathern. All rights reserved, including the right to reproduce
this book or portions thereof in any form. For information,
address: Ivan R. Dee, Publisher, 1332 North Halsted Street,
Chicago 60622. Manufactured in the United States of America
and printed on acid-free paper.

www.ivanrdee.com

Library of Congress Cataloging-in-Publication Data:
Strathern, Paul, 1940–
    Tolstoy in 90 minutes / Paul Strathern.
        p. cm.
    Includes bibliographical references and index.
    ISBN-13: 978-1-56663-693-3 (cloth : alk. paper)
    ISBN-10: 1-56663-693-0 (cloth : alk. paper)
    ISBN-13: 978-1-56663-692-6 (pbk. : alk. paper)
    ISBN-10: 1-56663-692-2 (pbk. : alk. paper)
    1. Tolstoy, Leo, graf, 1828–1910. 2. Authors, Russian—
19th century—Biography. I. Title. II. Title: Tolstoy in ninety
minutes. III. Series: Strathern, Paul, 1940– Great writers in
90 minutes.
PG3385.S86 2006
891.73'3—dc22
[B]
                                        2006019764

Contents

TOLSTOY IN 90 MINUTES

Introduction

Homer, Dante, Shakespeare, Goethe, and Tolstoy are generally reckoned as the five transcendent writers of the Western literary tradition. Of these, Tolstoy was the most evidently autobiographical, as well as being the most modern, which means that we know much more about him than the others. What emerges is a very odd individual indeed (making one suspect that the other four may well have been rather more unusual than the usual figures presented to us by tradition).

Tolstoy may have developed a monstrous talent, but at the same time he also developed a monstrous ego. That is not to say he was anything so trivial as vain. On the contrary, he strove to be humble—despite the fact that humility was completely alien to his nature. Tolstoy's ego was of the domineering sort: he wanted to tell everyone precisely how he thought they ought to conduct their lives, what they ought to believe, and ultimately what life was all about.

This element in his character he just about managed to keep in check in his early works. Later, the sheer power of his great talent just managed to absorb this egotistic flaw. Just. The Old Testament prophet in his nature occasionally overcomes the superb writer, even in his masterpieces *War and Peace* and *Anna Karenina,* but this seems forgivable when one is confronted with the plethora of his literary talents in full spate. It can be seen as just another aspect of his nature—maybe even a necessary one. An artist of such vast vision is perhaps bound to include a moral vision. The unbalanced aspect—the hectoring bore who fleetingly emerges—makes one appreciate the difficulty of achieving constant balance when one is possessed of such gargantuan talents. Certainly the latter stages of *War and Peace*, with the emergence of war over peace, seem to deserve at least a modicum of righteous anger. Refined literary taste may prefer to see brutality and stupidity on such a scale merely presented, with final judgment left to the reader, but Tolstoy in his wisdom thought otherwise. He had his theory of history to propound. And all this appears acceptable—just a minor flaw—in his masterpiece.

But in his later years this flaw—this monstrous ego—would all but destroy his creative talent. The opinionated Tolstoy had much to say about the world he saw around him while Russia certainly needed someone to speak out about its colossal injustices. And this role he valiantly fulfilled. But by this stage his vision of the world had narrowed to that of a saint: the only hope for the inhabitants of Holy Russia was for them all to aspire to holiness, like himself. His utopia would have reduced the country to a land of Christ-like pilgrims and simple peasants. Curiously, this was not the aberration of one great writer, driven to distraction by compassion for his nation's suffering masses. His great contemporary Dostoevsky ended up by adopting a very similar vision in the last years of his life. Extraordinarily, this vision would persist through the largely godless following century of Russia's history and into our own twenty-first century: Solzhenitsyn's solution to Russia's problems bears a marked similarity to that held by his two great predecessors.

But we should never forget: before reaching this nadir of rant, Tolstoy's life was a long and eventful spiritual journey which produced some of the greatest literature known to humanity.

Tolstoy's Life and Works

Leo Nikolaevich Tolstoy was born on August 28 (September 29 new calendar), 1828, at the family estate of Yasnaya Polyana, just over a hundred miles south of Moscow in the province of Tula. He was the fourth son of Count Nikolaevich Ilyich Tolstoy, a member of one of the leading Russian families, several members of which had distinguished themselves in the diplomatic corps. Young Leo's earliest years were characterized by an atmosphere of death and the frequent moving of home. His mother, Princess Volkonskaya, died before he reached the age of two; the family then moved to Moscow, where his father would die seven years later, whereupon his grandmother became his guardian for less than a year before she too died. In 1841 Tolstoy and his four siblings moved to Kazan, a provincial city nearly five hundred miles east of Moscow, where they were looked after by an aunt. Despite this frequent moving and the deaths of close family members, Tolstoy would remember his childhood as a happy period, filled with many idyllic scenes of upper-class Russian life:

> When we arrived at the Kalina wood we found the carriage already there and, surpassing our highest expectations, a one-horse cart in the middle of which sat the butler. From under the hay in it peeped a samovar, a pail with an ice-cream mold, and some other attractive bundles and boxes. There could be no mistake: it meant tea in the open air, with ices and fruit. At the sight of the cart we loudly expressed our delight, for to drink tea in the woods, on the grass, and in general somewhere where no one had ever drunk tea before was considered a great treat.

Young Leo was educated at home by private tutors before going to the *gymnasium* (upper school) in Kazan when he was fourteen. Around this time he had his first sexual experience, an event that assumed a deep significance. Monastic life in Kazan must have been rather easygoing, for according to Tolstoy there was a room in one of the monasteries where a prostitute was housed, and he was taken there by his older brother Sergey. When Tolstoy had lost his virginity to the woman, he remembered, "I sat down afterward at the foot of the woman's bed and cried." He was so overcome with shame and guilt that he would remain chaste for some time to come.

In 1844, at the age of sixteen, Tolstoy enrolled at the University of Kazan, whose rector was the world-famous mathematician Nikolai Lobachevsky, founder of non-Euclidian geometry. Following the accession of Tsar Nicholas I in the 1820s, Lobachevsky had introduced many reforms at Kazan University, raising its educational standards. But by now Nicholas I had become a reactionary autocrat, who would be remembered as "the emperor who froze Russia for thirty years," and Kazan University had lapsed into provincialism. Tolstoy initially studied oriental languages with the intention of entering the diplomatic service, but owing to his lack of application he was obliged to switch to the easier course in law. Like so many young gentlemen, he liked to get drunk, he liked to ride his horse, and he liked to dress up in smart clothes; but underneath it all he remained an intense young man, much preoccupied with the state of his soul.

It was now that Tolstoy began reading the eighteenth-century Romantic writer and philosopher Jean-Jacques Rousseau, whose words struck him with all the force of a revelation. "I thought I was reading my own mind," he would recall. Among other works, he read Rousseau's didactic novel *Émile*, which concerns itself with the way we should be educated in order to become fully realized human beings. This famously opens, "Everything is good as it leaves the hands of the Author of things; everything degenerates in the hands of man." Later Rousseau declares that all previous education has been faulty because it did not take into account what we are. At one point he recounts the travails of a young Savoyard peasant who becomes ordained as a priest before he has matured sufficiently to question the nature of his vows. Although filled with piety, he finds himself plagued by his inability to keep his vow of chastity. Intense and perplexed, he searches for the truth of his life. He decides, "One's first duty is towards oneself." Nevertheless he recognizes that his conscience is the true voice of his soul; this is the "Divine instinct, the immortal voice from heaven."

Tolstoy was racked with religious doubt and the problems of faith; he would study the catechism and pray to God, yet at the same time admit to himself, "I saw clearly that the whole catechism was false." Like so many young men of his age, he was driven by contradictory impulses. He still wished to enter government service, yet he was beginning to feel that the entire system of government in Russia was hopelessly unjust. Part of him longed for spiritual purity, but he frequently felt overcome by lust and visited gypsy prostitutes. He often acted with the arrogance of his aristocratic lineage, yet he could not but help feel for the plight of the impoverished people he saw around him. Ironically, despite being a member of the landed gentry, his family was an impoverished branch of the Tolstoys, and while a student he often found himself lacking in funds compared with his aristocratic young peers.

In 1847 Tolstoy left Kazan University without having taken a degree, officially because of "ill health and domestic circumstances." In fact he was hospitalized for a time, during which he underwent painful mercury treatment for venereal disease. This only accentuated his tendency toward self-loathing and his determination to live a pure and proper life. He now returned to run the family estate at Yasnaya Polyana. Instead of wearing a Christian cross about his neck, he took to wearing a medallion stamped with a portrait of his hero Rousseau. With Rousseau's example in mind he determined to educate himself properly; he would also seek to improve the condition of the serfs who worked on the estate as virtual slaves.

We have a good insight into the nineteen-year-old Tolstoy's mind at this time because he started keeping a diary—concerned not so much with what he did but with what he thought. Now and for the rest of his life he would keep a diary in which he examined his thoughts, his principles, and his failings. "I would be the un-happiest of men," he records at one point, "if I could not find a purpose for my life—a purpose both general and useful—useful because my im-mortal soul when fully mature will pass naturally into a higher existence and one that is appropri-ate to it. So my whole life will be a constant and active striving to achieve this one purpose." He draws up rules of conduct but constantly falls short of them: "It is easier to write ten volumes of philosophy than to put a single precept into practice." He starts reading Dickens; he takes to wearing a loose canvas smock with slippers and bare legs in an attempt to live out Rous-seau's "back to nature" ideas; he spends hours lying under a tree "communing with nature."

17

Inevitably he soon became bored with living in the depths of the country dressed in a nightgown. In 1848 he began making trips to Moscow, where he went on gambling, drinking, and whoring sprees; in between times he read in the newspapers of the short-lived uprisings that were taking place in cities all over Europe during this "year of revolutions."

In the following year Tolstoy decided to renew his formal education, registering at the university in St. Petersburg to study law. But he left after just two terms and continued to live a haphazard and dissipated life, running up heavy gambling debts in St. Petersburg, Moscow, and the provincial capital of Tula. But between times he continued reading, and in 1851 he embarked upon his first serious attempt to write, producing "A Short History of Yesterday," an apprentice piece which attempts to describe in detail the events that take place during a single day. This remained uncompleted, and he turned to another literary project—a description of events from his childhood—which seemed better adapted to his talents. But in April 1851 he broke off once more and decided to join his brother Nikolai, who was serving as an army officer in the Caucasus.

Here Tolstoy saw action when he joined his brother on an expedition against rebel tribesmen. During the winter in Tiflis (now in Georgia), Tolstoy completed *Childhood,* writing in the early mornings or evenings after a day's hunting with his brother. The manuscript was rewritten three times, with meticulous attention to detail. In his diary he noted: "Without regret, I must destroy all unclear passages, anything verbose or irrelevant, in a word, everything that is unsatisfactory, no matter how fine it may be in itself." Eventually he sent the manuscript to *The Contemporary*, the leading literary magazine in St. Petersburg. The editor, the poet Nikolai Nekrasov, recognized the talent in this manuscript by an unknown author who simply signed himself as L.N.T.; without further ado he decided to publish Tolstoy's story. From the opening lines of *Childhood* it is possible to discern Tolstoy's mature style in embryo, with its attention to telling detail, clarity, and assurance— much of which had been achieved by his constant meticulous rewriting. The author is plainly living his experiences as he recounts them, and manages to convey this so directly that the reader feels he is there:

> On the 12th August 18—, exactly three days after my tenth birthday, on which I received such wonderful presents, Karl Ivanych woke me up at seven in the morning by hitting a fly just above my head with a flap of blue sugar-bag paper fastened to a stick. He did this so awkwardly that he caught the little picture of my patron-saint, which hung from the top of my oak bedstead, and the dead fly fell right on my head.

The words do not come between the reader and the scene; they appear to convey Tolstoy's heightened consciousness itself. At one point he describes what is happening to him as he writes:

> So many past memories arise when one tries to recall the features of a beloved being that one sees those features dimly through the memories as if through tears. They are the

tears of imagination. When I try to recall my mother as she was at that time I can only picture her brown eyes . . . her neck just below the place where the short curls grew, her embroidered white collar, and the delicate dry hand which so often caressed me.

Not all of *Childhood* is so surefooted and successful. The memories—especially of "Mama"—are an imaginative reconstruction of an event he wishes to see; they are created memories, and in the process the twenty-three-year-old writer forces his more mature perceptions into the vision of the child. At other times the clarity of vision is not even Tolstoy's own, betraying influences that he has not yet fully absorbed; a few passages are almost a copy of the child's perceptions in David Copperfield.

But the overall effect is impressive, and this first published piece certainly caught the eye of some superior figures. Dostoevsky, in exile in Siberia, was more than impressed, and Turgenev was full of praise for the mysterious L.N.T., declaring, "When this wine is mature it will be a drink fit for the gods." Tolstoy himself was over-joyed to see a highly favorable review of *Childhood*; he now had no doubt about what he wanted to do with his life—he would be a writer. He immediately began planning a series of stories and sketches, but he was unable to bring these to completion for he had volunteered to join the army and was now a cadet in the Caucasus. Army life led Tolstoy into a number of adventures, during which he saw action several times, on one occasion nearly being killed by a grenade, on another narrowly evading capture by Chechen rebels. By 1854 he had been commissioned and the Crimean War had broken out, with the British and the French landing an expeditionary force in southern Russia. Tolstoy spent several periods at Sebastopol while the war raged all around, with a series of chaotic battles and much needless slaughter. Despite this, he and his fellow officers found time in their garrisons for carousing and gambling, and in between times Tolstoy completed "The Raid," which was published in *The Contemporary* and began what would become his *Sebastopol Sketches*.

"The Raid" is a long story based on a military action in which Tolstoy had taken part in the preceding year. He describes the heroism, as well as the quirks, of the soldiers involved. Each of the different characters comes alive—for the simple reason that they are each in turn fully and psychologically inhabited by the author. They are, in essence, each different aspects of himself. Here his self-disgust is able to fall away as he lives out the individual lives with their disparate frailties. Yet "The Raid" also had its moral purpose, with its author declaring defiantly that he was "more interested to know in what way and under the influence of what feeling one soldier kills another than to know how the armies were arranged at Austerlitz or Borodino." Unfortunately this moral aspect of Tolstoy's story would fall foul of the censors, and only a truncated version of "The Raid" appeared in *The Contemporary*.

Tolstoy's *Sebastopol Sketches* derive from his experiences during the siege of the Crimean seaport and its major Russian naval base. The sketches are experimental in character, yet despite his use of novel literary devices the force and clarity of the words remain undiminished. The first sketch, "Sebastopol in December," evokes the scene with superb clarity. This is already the writing of a master, sure of his effects; each detail evokes the larger world, with not a word too many:

> The activity of day is beginning gradually to replace the quiet of night: here some soldiers with clanking muskets pass to relieve the guard, there a doctor is already hurrying to the hospital, and there a soldier, having crept out of his dug-out, washes his weather-beaten face with icy water and then turning to the reddening horizon says his prayers, rapidly crossing himself; a creaking Tartar cart drawn by camels crawls past on its way to the cemetery to bury the blood-stained dead with which it is loaded almost to the top.

Side by side the horror and the exoticism of the scene are conveyed: this is the universal squalor of war and death, and yet the scene belongs utterly to one particular time and place. The sketch goes on to portray the comradeship and heroism of the simple soldiers manning a gun battery under fire from the nearby besieging enemy. Although the men are in danger of their lives, they still manage to laugh, quarrel, and play cards in their dugout. Tolstoy takes the daring decision to describe the scenes in Sebastopol in the second person singular. This device is not used obtrusively and serves to draw the reader subtly into the scenes he describes, at the same time letting him into the conversation the author is having with himself: "It is impossible for some feeling of heroism and pride not to penetrate your soul at the thought that you, too, are in Sebastopol, and for the blood not to run faster in your veins."

According to one story, when these words were read by Tsar Alexander II he was deeply moved by their patriotism and is said to have ordered, "Guard well the life of that young man." The second sketch, "Sebastopol in May," would end with the words: "The hero of my tale, whom I love with all the strength of my soul, the hero I have tried to reproduce in all his glory, who always has been, and always will be admirable, is the truth." Tolstoy would earnestly try to adhere to these words throughout his writing life; but such a literary credo was too much for the censor. Despite Tolstoy's patriotism and the tsar's benign encouragement, "Sebastopol in May" was heavily censored of all "anti-patriotic" material—the public had to be protected from the squalid and bloody truth of what was happening at the front in the Crimean War.

In 1856 a peace treaty was concluded between Russia, Britain, and France; with the ending of the Crimean War, Tolstoy left the army and returned to St. Petersburg, where he was greeted with acclaim as the new up-and-coming writer of Russia. By this time it was widely agreed among the intellectuals of St. Petersburg that Russian society was in desperate need of reform; Tolstoy was in deep sympathy with such sentiments but found himself unable to take sides in the petty squabbles among the different intellectual factions. He quarreled with Nekrasov and could only feel contempt for Turgenev and his liberal friends who supported gradual reform—their stance appeared to be little more than a fashionable pose. On the other hand, Tolstoy found himself utterly opposed to those of the left wing who advocated revolution—for Tolstoy their ungodliness and longing for violence was contrary to all his deeply held humanitarian principles. In the end he grew tired of being lionized and dragged into petty intellectual squabbles, and left for his country estate at Yasnaya Polyana. But the ideas circulating in St. Petersburg had affected him more deeply than he realized. He was now convinced that the present system of government in Russia was wrong, and he determined to do what he could to alleviate the sufferings it inflicted. Upon his return to the countryside he determined to liberate the serfs on his estate, though nothing came of this for the time being.

In the following year Tolstoy traveled to Western Europe with the aim of completing his education with the Grand Tour that was undertaken by so many aristocratic young men of the period. Having patched up his quarrels with Turgenev and Nekrasov, he accompanied them to Paris, where they visited a variety of brothels and indulged in "debauches." Tolstoy also witnessed a public execution by guillotine. Despite having witnessed much slaughter in the Crimea, he was profoundly shocked by this event:

> When I saw the head part from the body and how it thumped separately into the box, I understood, not with my mind, but with my whole being that no theory of the reasonableness of our present progress could justify this deed, and that though everyone from the creation of the world, on whatever theory, had held it to be necessary, I knew it would be unnecessary and bad; and therefore the arbiter of what is good and evil is not what people say and do, nor is it progress, but is my heart and I.

Although these words were written at a much later date, such feelings were already beginning to stir within him. He wished to accept the truth only as he saw it. His thinking would be independent of theory, progress, history, or "what people say"—he would respond only to "my heart and I." Rousseau's "conscience" was evolving within him: he wished to view the world with the same clarity of eye as he wrote about it. But such "truth" remained very much an un-achieved aim, and his attempts to be honest to himself still left him very much a bewildered young man. At this stage in his life his opinions were only gradually resolving their contradictions, his thoughts remaining very much in turmoil: "The Law of man—what nonsense! The truth is that the state is a conspiracy designed not only to exploit, but above all to corrupt its citizens."

After Paris he traveled on alone to Switzerland by rail, a mode of transport which he found artificial and boring. He wrote to Turgenev: "For God's sake travel wherever you like but only not by rail. The railroad is to a journey what a brothel is to love: just as convenient, but also just as humanly mechanical and deadly monotonous."

After traveling through Germany he returned home and wrote a number of stories based on his experiences in Europe. Typical of these is *Lucerne*, based on an incident during Tolstoy's stay in Switzerland, recorded in his diary. While walking about one evening in Lucerne, Tolstoy came across a poor little Tyrolean street singer. He was so touched by the plight of this impoverished, misshapen man that he invited him back to sing outside his hotel, the Schweitzerhof, one of the grandest in the city. No one gave the singer any money, and eventually Tolstoy took it upon himself to invite the singer in for a meal. This only resulted in a number of embarrassing scenes, with the hotel guests and servants making it quite plain that they despised the humble Tyrolean. Afterward Tolstoy parted from the singer and paced the darkened streets in a turmoil, demanding of himself: "What is it I so ardently desire? I do not know. . . . My God! What am I? Where am I going? Where am I?" These words were recorded by Tolstoy in his diary, but the story he later wrote would also end on a didactic, questioning note.

> Which is more civilized, which more of a barbarian: the lord who stamped away from the table in a huff at the sight of the singer's threadbare suit, who refused to pay him for

his work with the millionth part of his fortune . . . or the little singer who has been out on the road for twenty years, with two sous in his pocket . . . [who] has now gone off, humiliated, almost driven away, tired, hungry and ashamed, to sleep in some nameless place on a heap of rotting straw?

These and other stories that Tolstoy wrote at this time were attacked by the critics for being far too indulgent and subjective. They were disturbed by the naked obtrusiveness of Tolstoy's opinions, which had not been absorbed into art. At the same time he began writing a novel entitled *The Cossacks*, which was intended to capture his earlier life and experiences in the Caucasus. Here the sheer force and verve of the material appeared to overcome the opinionated author, forcing him to employ all his artistry and talent. But Tolstoy eventually tired of simply creating literature: this was not what he intended to write at all. As a result, he turned away from trying to write literary works and immersed himself in running his estate at Yasnaya Polyana. Thus

Tolstoy's life and literary career might well have ended, for one day while out hunting he was attacked by a bear, and was lucky to escape with his life.

Tolstoy now busied himself with trying to improve the lot of his serfs. Initially he concentrated on education, setting up a school where their children could be taught to read and write. What for? one might well ask. What use was literacy to a dirt-poor peasant forced to work all hours in the fields for his master? Tolstoy countered such questions by insisting that the peasants would soon begin to enjoy reading "for its own sake." A tutor hired to teach at Tolstoy's peasant school recalled arriving to find the children swarming around an amiable man with a large black beard dressed in a peasant costume, apparently the leading serf of the village. This turned out to be Tolstoy himself, who had now "gone native" and was immersing himself in the life of his serfs, though still returning each evening to eat dinner and sleep in his own large house. When he encountered one of his serfs while walking in the fields, he was likely to embrace and kiss him in a Rousseau-like gesture of fraternal love. "Their beards smell wonderfully of spring," he wrote to one of his relatives, a lady-in-waiting at the tsar's court. His interest in the peasant women was more frankly sensual, and when he came across one in the woods he might "seduce" her. He eventually became besotted with Aksinya Bazykina, the twenty-three-year-old wife of one of his serfs. "I'm in love as never before in my life," he wrote in his diary. "She's very pretty. . . . Today in the big wood. I'm a fool. A beast. Her neck is red from the sun." This infatuation would eventually settle into a slightly more permanent relationship, resulting in a son, who in turn would also be educated at Tolstoy's serf school before becoming one of the estate's coachmen. Such events had long been accepted on Russian estates during tsarist times: Tolstoy's father had gained a coachman under identical circumstances.

When summer came, the little pupils of Tolstoy's school were needed in the fields to bring in the harvest, which required everyone to work all hours from sunrise until the night dew settled. By now Tolstoy had concluded that the education in his small country school was lacking in method, and in July 1859 he set off for Germany to study the latest educational theories being put into practice in their schools. He had another reason for visiting Germany: his brother Nikolai was now ill in the last stages of tuberculosis, and had left Russia to stay at the Prussian health resort of Soden.

Many of the schools that Tolstoy visited in Germany were basic in the extreme: "a prayer said for the King, regular caning, everything learned by rote, producing nothing but cowed and frightened children, morally deformed." But a number of German educators had thought long and hard about the best method of teaching young children, and Tolstoy was lucky enough to meet a nephew of Friedrich Froebel, the founder of the kindergarten system. Never one to accept anything he was told, Tolstoy was soon giving Froebel's nephew the benefit of his own educational experience and what he had in mind. According to Froebel's nephew, "Progress in Russia, he told me, must come out of public education, which among us will give better results than in Germany, because the Russian masses are not yet spoiled by education."

Tolstoy had a deep belief in "the Russian masses." The peasantry, untainted by education, barely touched even by civilization in their state of serfdom, in Tolstoy's view were akin to Rousseau's noble savage. But the innocence he saw in such noble savages was essentially a reflection of his own innocence, with its own unclouded vision. Tolstoy was not innocent in himself, far from it, but his insistence on viewing the world through his own eyes often left him as untouched by the ways of civilization as his serfs. He was learning to see things as no other, his unclouded eye discovering how to detect the subtlest of nuances.

Nowhere would this aspect of Tolstoy's character come into play more evidently than when he visited his brother at Soden, and later at Hyeres in the south of France, where Nikolai was moved so that he could benefit from the more temperate climate. Here Tolstoy went through the profoundly moving experience of watching

Nikolai die. As Tolstoy recorded in his diary: "He didn't say that he felt death approaching, but I know he followed its every step, and surely knew what still remained to him of life." Tolstoy could now see with such clarity that he seemed to see inside people; such was his intentness and empathy that he appeared to live their lives for them. As he wrote of his brother Nikolai: "All who knew and saw his last minutes say: 'How wonderfully peacefully and calmly he died,' but I know how frightfully agonizing it was, for not a single feeling escaped me." With his words Tolstoy did not create character, he *inhabited* it.

During the funeral of his brother, Tolstoy conceived of writing "a practical Gospel, a materialist life of Christ." On his return to Russia he once again began producing books—but these were not literature, they were textbooks, written with simplicity and clarity, for use in schools. He even founded a magazine, called *Yasnaya Polyana*, in which he propounded his pedagogical ideas. But his views on education were not always viewed sympathetically, even among his fellow intellectuals. Turgenev, who was at the height of his powers and renown, took exception to Tolstoy's opinions, especially when he remarked about Turgenev educating his natural daughter to become a gentlewoman with a well-developed sense of charity by having her take in ragged clothes from the poor and mend them. Tolstoy called this "a hypocritical farce"; Turgenev repudiated this remark, and Tolstoy challenged him to a duel. In Tolstoy's reaction there was an element of jealousy: he may have seen through others, but he did not always see through himself, despite all his agonized self-questioning. Fortunately his challenge came to nothing—or Russia might have lost two more of its finest writers to pistol wounds. (The great poet Pushkin had died in a duel just twenty-four years earlier, in 1837; four years after this the poet Lermontov had suffered a similar fate.)

In 1861 the new tsar Alexander II had issued a decree liberating the serfs, adding the proviso that the owners should grant each serf sufficient land to support himself and his family. The provincial governor of Tula appointed Tolstoy as Arbiter of Peace for his district, with the task of arbitrating in the many inevitable disputes that arose from the liberation. To the indignation of the local gentry, Tolstoy tended to side with the serfs in these arguments over land, though his decisions were usually overturned when the landowner appealed to the higher court.

The tsarist secret police had been keeping an eye on Tolstoy ever since the censoring of his second Sebastopol sketch. Acting upon stories circulating about his serf school and its advanced European ideas, and a rumor that he now had a secret printing press hidden in his house, they decided to act. Carefully biding their time until Tolstoy himself had left for a summer holiday, they raided Yasnaya Polyana, turning the place upside down and even dredging the pond. Nothing seriously incriminating was found, and when Tolstoy returned he was furious. He dashed off an angry letter to his aunt Alexandra, a lady-in-waiting at the court:

> If you will recall my political attitude you will know that always, and especially since my love for the school, I have been entirely indif-

ferent to the government, and even more in-
different to the present liberals whom I scorn
with all my soul. Now I can no longer say
this. I possess bitterness and revulsion, almost hatred for that dear Government.

It appeared that Tolstoy's political attitude was
hardening, but this did not mean that he es-
poused the extreme revolutionary cause. His was
the disgust of an aristocrat for his fellow aristocrats who ruled so ineptly. In spirit he might have
been virtually an anarchist (albeit a highly prin-
cipled, religious one), but in the flesh he remained an independent-minded member of the
upper classes. He may have lived among his
serfs, but he retained strong social links with the
privileged few, the aristocrats and prosperous
middle-class landowners.

Among the latter were the Behrs family, who
spent the summer at their estate thirty-five miles
from Yasnaya Polyana. On a visit to the Behrs,
Tolstoy became attracted to their second daughter, the seventeen-year-old Sofia. He had known
Sofia on and off since she was a child, but his

regard for her as a woman was to be character-istically impulsive. They met in early August; he followed her when her family returned to Moscow in late August, and proposed to her in mid-September. After being accepted, Tolstoy decided that they should be completely open with each other; before they were married, he insisted that Sofia read his personal diaries. These contained all of Tolstoy's secrets, especially his darker sexual ones, including details of his visits to whores from Kazan to Paris, his early venereal disease, his exploits with gypsy women in the Caucasus, his romps with his serfs, and even his longer-lasting infatuation with his serf Aksinya, which had only recently cooled. The innocent Sofia was reduced to tears, later writing in her own diary: "I don't think I ever recovered from the shock of reading the diaries when I was engaged to him. I can still remember the agonizing pangs of jealousy, the horror of that first appalling experience of male depravity."

Yet astonishingly Sofia forgave her Leo for the long list of misdemeanors she had read about in such detail, and still agreed to marry him. Just six days after Tolstoy's proposal, he and Sofia were married.

Tolstoy was to find stability in his marriage to Sofia, and soon their first child, a son named Sergei, was born at Yasnaya Polyana. The relationship between Leo and Sofia was intense, rendered even more so by the fact that he insisted she should continue reading his diaries as he went on writing them. These included all his more intimate thoughts and often hurtful secret feelings; but Tolstoy thrived in this atmosphere of openness as well as the redemption Sofia bestowed on him when she forgave him his misdeeds. Writing was Tolstoy's confession: he could be nothing other than true to what he saw, what he felt, what he thought, what he sensed, both in himself and in others.

Sofia's blessing both absolved him and at the same time condoned his utter honesty. In this atmosphere Tolstoy once more settled down to write. But this time it was no longer pedagogical articles, educational tracts, or even didactic stories illustrating his principles and opinions. This time he turned once more to what he was best at, writing literature. His initial motive was not a new self-understanding but the need for money. Under his somewhat erratic husbandry, the estate was generating little cash, and he now had a family to support. To begin with he embarked upon another rewriting of *The Cossacks*, finally completing it. Before this Tolstoy had been a highly talented writer, but with *The Cossacks* he moved into a different sphere: it was his first masterpiece.

The story is of a young aristocrat named Olenin, who closely resembles certain aspects of Tolstoy's own character ten years earlier:

> Olenin was a youth who had never completed his university course, never served anywhere (having only a nominal post in some government office or other), who had squandered half his fortune and had reached the age of twenty-four without having done anything or even chosen a career.

Disillusioned with sophisticated life in Moscow, Olenin sets off for the Caucasus. There he lives among the Cossacks, whose natural way of life and traditional attitudes revive his taste for life. In the course of the novel we are introduced to a cast of well-realized characters. We meet the tall, handsome, twenty-year-old Lukashka:

> His ample Circassian coat was torn in some places, his cap was on the back of his head Chechen fashion, and his leggings had slipped below his knees. His clothing was not rich, but he wore it with that peculiar Cossack foppishness. Everything on a real brave is ample, ragged, and neglected, only his weapons are costly.

We follow him on a boar hunt and watch Olenin's awkward attempts to befriend him. Olenin is drawn to the redoubtable old hunter Yeroshka, but the old man's quaint way of speech only serves to emphasize the gulf that separates them. Olenin also falls in love with the "devil's woman," Maryanka, but his timid approach fails to move her. He soon realizes that despite the enlivening effect these people have on him he can never really become a part of them. Yet he learns from his experiences, learns about

himself, and ponders his way to certain conclu-
sions:

> Happiness is to live for others. That is clear.
> In man there exists the need for happiness,
> therefore it is legitimate. In satisfying this de-
> sire in a selfish manner, that is to say in seek-
> ing for himself fame and riches, it can only
> happen that circumstances will become such
> as will make it impossible for him to satisfy
> all his desires. Therefore these desires are ille-
> gitimate, but the need of happiness itself, that
> is not wrong. What then are those desires
> which can always be satisfied in spite of ex-
> ternal conditions? Love, the sacrifice of one-
> self.

Even here Tolstoy could not rid himself of the
need to philosophize, but in *The Cossacks* his ru-
minating is more integrated, more part of the
story, which despite beautifully realized but
lengthy descriptive passages has a strong narrative drive. The reader quickly becomes interested
in the Cossacks, involved in what is happening,

keen to know how situations will be resolved, what will happen next. Unlike previous descriptions of the exotic Caucasus by authors such as Pushkin and Lermontov, this place and its people are not obscured by mists of romanticism. This is a harsh, difficult mountain land, at the very edges of the civilized world, inhabited by a primitive people who have their own integrity. Although Olenin realizes he can never overcome barriers of race, culture, and class that separate him from these people, by the end of his stay he understands the full import of what he has learned from them. When Yeroshka casts aspersions on the Russian officers and their doctors, dismissing them as "phonys," "Olenin did not begin to reply. He was in all too much agreement that everything was phony in the world in which he lived and to which he was returning."

When Olenin rides off in the cart taking him back home, Yeroshka yells after him, "Farewell, my boy. Farewell. I won't forget you." But when Olenin turns around for a last glance at the world he is leaving, "Old Yeroshka was talking to Maryanka, evidently about his own affairs,

and neither the old man nor the girl were looking in his direction any more."

When *The Cossacks* was published in 1863 it
initially caused little stir. Aunt Alexandra wrote
from Moscow about reactions among her circle:
"My friends, Boris and others, were enchanted;
others criticized *The Cossacks* for a certain
crudeness which, they say, inhibits the aesthetic
response. . . . While one is reading, the book is
satisfying, a very accurate and truthful photo-
graph, but when one has finished, one is left
thirsting for something bigger, on a more elevated level." Fortunately the leading newspaper
of Russia's most "Europeanized" city, the *St. Petersburg News,* was quick to spot the book's
worth, proclaiming *The Cossacks* to be "a capital achievement in Russian literature, able to sus-
tain comparison with the greatest novels of the
last decade." Even Turgenev, now living in exile
in Paris, was moved to declare, "I have read *The
Cossacks* and was carried away"—though he
couldn't resist a snide comment about the semi-
autobiographical Olenin: "To mark the contrast
between civilization and primitive, unspoiled na-

ture, there was no necessity to trot out this individual who is incessantly preoccupied with himself, boring and unhealthy."

Tolstoy seems to have taken Aunt Alexandra's advice, for he now set about writing a much bigger, more ambitious novel whose subject matter was far more elevated than life among the Cossacks. It would be concerned with nothing less than the entirety of Russian society. Tolstoy began writing his new novel in 1863, and it was more than six years before he had completed, and rewritten many times, the work that would become known as *War and Peace*.

The book opens in July 1805 at the salon of Madame Scherer, a lady-in-waiting to the tsarina. The atmosphere of this aristocratic salon is realized in all its superficial elegance as the guests converse, switching with ease from Russian to French. Here we are introduced to the young Prince Andrei Bolkonsky, who dislikes the falsity of social life, as well as to the ingenuous, bumbling Pierre Bezukhov, who has just returned from Switzerland. These two fully realized leading characters also cleverly represent the different sides of Tolstoy's character. The conversation is of Napoleon, who has now conquered a large part of Europe and threatens to overrun even more. Prince Andrei appears impressed by the heroic aspects of Napoleon and his conquests, and cannot refrain from quoting Napoleon's words at his recent coronation: "God has given this to me, beware he who dares to touch it." Others point to Napoleon's cruelties, his arrogance, and his ruthlessnesss in kidnapping and murdering the Duc d'Enghien, the royalist he suspected of being behind a conspiracy to assassinate him. To the consternation of the hostess and her distinguished guests, Pierre interrupts: "The execution of the Duc d'Enghien was a political necessity, and it seems to me that Napoleon showed greatness of soul by not fearing to take on himself the whole responsibility of that deed." Pierre is impressed by Napoleon's soul, Andrei by his heroism—already the difference between the two of them becomes clear, and a significant strand of the novel is taken up with the development and transformation of these two different ways of looking at the world.

War and Peace covers some fifteen hundred pages, which are divided into four volumes, followed by two epilogues. It is both a novel, describing the rich and varied social life of Russia, and a fictionalized history of the unfolding events from 1805 to Napoleon's invasion of Russia and beyond, culminating in 1814. The vast cast of characters consists of fictional and real figures—ranging from peasants and soldiers to Napoleon and the tsar—whose lives and interactions are woven together to form the overall narrative tapestry.

The first epilogue draws together many of the loose ends left by the narrative, pointing to the future of the characters involved. The second epilogue consists of an essay outlining the philosophy of history that the novel is intended to illustrate. This is the bones, where the novel itself is the flesh. Fortunately Tolstoy's supreme novelistic skills ensure that the flesh of the novel has a vivid life of its own, which seldom appears determined by the somewhat unconvincing fatalistic philosophy that he could not refrain from tacking on at the end.

As we have seen, there was always a strong didactic ingredient in Tolstoy's creative impulse. But this element should not simply be dismissed as an aberration, as is so often the case. It was the guiding force that enabled him to shepherd such a large range of characters through the differing development of their lives. Such a guiding force is perhaps necessary even for a supreme writer attempting to create something so complex as an entire world of characters and events. In the twentieth century James Joyce would use a similar device in his novel *Ulysses*, incorporating the irrelevant myth of Ulysses as a structure on which to place his myriad bricks of Dublin life. Tolstoy believed that life had a meaning, and that this meaning was moral, hence it is entirely natural that he infused his novel with it. Joyce had no such belief, using the Ulysses myth for purely aesthetic purposes, comparing it to a bridge over which he marched his cast of characters, a structure that could safely be removed once the novel was completed. Tolstoy could never have similarly removed his beliefs from

50

War and Peace: they were his very life, and their moral force is what breathes life into his characters, into their successes and failures as human beings, into their unfolding development and fate. We should just be thankful that he left the exposition of his philosophy to the epilogue of *War and Peace*, so that we can read the novel itself unhampered by the author's preconceptions and can simply ignore "the message" at the end if we so choose.

An example of Tolstoy's moral development of his characters—his depiction of their spiritual journey, if you like—may be seen in the life of Prince Andrei Bolkonsky as it unfolds in the first volume. At the outset he is a proud young man, fully convinced of his untried belief in heroism. At the end of the volume we see him at the battle of Austerlitz, where the Russian and Austrian forces faced the French army in Austrian territory some seventy miles north of Vienna. In the battle Andrei shows considerable bravery, leaping from his horse to seize the standard from a fallen officer, and encouraging the batallion in a charge toward the French lines. But in the midst of this he is wounded by enemy fire:

> It seemed to him as though one of the soldiers near him hit him on the head with the full swing of a bludgeon. It hurt a little, but the worst of it was that the pain distracted him and prevented his seeing what he had been looking at.
>
> "What's this? Am I falling? My legs are giving way," thought he, and fell on his back.

He passes out, and when he comes to:

> Above him there was now nothing but the sky—the lofty sky, not clear yet still immeasurably lofty, with great clouds gliding slowly across it. "How quiet, peaceful and solemn, not at all as like when I was charging," thought Andrei—"not like when we were charging, shouting and fighting. Not at all like the guns and the Frenchmen, with their frightened and angry faces: how differently do those clouds glide across the lofty infinite sky."

In his dreamy state, as he lies wounded on the battlefield, he wonders to himself how he has not noticed the lofty sky before, exclaiming to himself:

"And how happy I am to have found it at last! Yes! All is vanity, all falsehood, except that infinite sky. There is nothing, nothing, but that. But even it does not exist, there is nothing but quiet and peace. Thank God! . . . "

Tolstoy skillfully demonstrates the effect of this revelation—this moment of profound understanding—upon Andrei. He is discovered by French soldiers and carried on a stretcher, eventually finding himself in the presence of the victorious Napoleon, who is inspecting his Russian prisoners. Napoleon addresses Andrei:

"Well, and you young man," said he. "How do you feel, *mon brave*?" Though five minutes before Prince Andrei had been able to say a few words to the soldiers who were carrying him, now with his eyes fixed straight on

Napoleon, he was silent. . . . So insignificant at that moment seemed to him all the interests that engrossed Napoleon, so mean did his hero himself with his paltry vanity and joy in victory appear, compared to the lofty, equitable and kindly sky which he had seen and understood, that he could not answer him.

After his experience of the lofty sky, "everything seemed so futile and insignificant" compared with "the stern and solemn train of thought that weakness from loss of blood, suffering, and the nearness of death, aroused in him." These external details render Andrei's moment of truth all the more convincing. Even greatness personified—Napoleon himself—is convincingly belittled:

Looking into Napoleon's eyes Prince Andrei thought of the insignificance of greatness, the unimportance of life which no one could understand, and the still greater unimportance of death, the meaning of which no one alive could understand or explain.

54

Even in stating the impossibility of understanding life, Tolstoy manages to convey his belief that there *is* something to understand, that all that is happening has meaning. And even if one does not share Tolstoy's belief, one is nonetheless convinced that his characters come to the belief that they inhabit such a world. Such is the power of his writing that the bloody chaos of battle and the vain grandeur of Napoleon—conveyed with such compelling clarity—ring no more true than the spiritual experience of Prince Andrei as he lies wounded beneath the sky.

Where the first volume of *War and Peace* covers the six months from June to November 1805, the second volume covers six years—from 1806 to 1811—years of peace after the 1807 Treaty of Tilsit, before Napoleon's massive invasion of Russia in 1812. Amidst a succession of balls, salons, family meetings, and other public and private events we follow the fortunes of the main protagonists and their five families— the Bezukhovs (to which Pierre will belong), the Rostovs, the Bolkonskys (including Prince Andrei), the Kuragins, and the Drubetskoys.

Several of the characters in these families are modeled upon people close to Tolstoy. The emotionally complicated Princess Marie Bolkonsky, a figure who is depicted with considerable psychological insight and depth, was based upon Tolstoy's mother (or what he had heard of her, and imagined of her). The most striking of all the female characters, Natasha Rostov, was modeled upon Tatiana Behrs, the young sister of Tolstoy's wife Sofia. During the period when he was writing *War and Peace,* Tolstoy became close to his sister-in-law Tatiana, and she became his confidante, allowing him deep insight into her character. Perhaps because Tolstoy did not actually have an affair with Tatiana, he remained fascinated by her, and this fascination enlivens the character of Natasha, the central female figure in *War and Peace.* Despite this and other resemblances—his father, his grandfather, his aunt, and another sister-in-law each appear in some guise—the characters in *War and Peace* are all fully realized independent creations. This was to be no family album; it was intended to depict a full range of human temperaments.

At least in the "peace" sections of the novel, the milieu remains for the most part distinctly upper class, though there is much less of the restraint that characterized civilized society in Western European countries of the period. Tolstoy's characters would have suffocated in the world of Jane Austen's *Pride and Prejudice,* for instance. The social proceedings are enlivened by outbursts of distinctly Slavonic impulsiveness and reaction. There is no mistaking the behavior in the salons of Moscow for the overrefinement of contemporary Georgian Bath in England. Tolstoy's characters may have European manners, but they remain Russians, with their own norms of behavior, whose gradations Tolstoy conveys with consummate ease.

In contrasting Russian manners with those prevalent in Western Europe at the time, we are reminded of Tolstoy's behavior with the poor Tyrolean singer and the reactions of European guests at the Schweitzerhof Hotel, particularly that of the English lord. Of all the people whom Tolstoy disliked—and could never understand—the English were preeminent. Their unfeeling, unquestioning pragmatism, their utilitarianism, their ability to live easily with themselves, all this was the very antithesis of Tolstoy's anguished self-questioning.

Slavonic manners were not without their own subtleties, even if their ingenuousness and enthusiasms could make Western manners appear effete. Such earnestness and frequent intensity was not without its lighter moments and even humor, but it made it easier for Tolstoy's characters to discuss—with themselves or with others—any worries they might have had about their life or their "soul." Amidst all the glitter of the social scene, Tolstoy's preoccupation with spiritual matters was never far below the surface.

It is Pierre who eventually emerges as the leading character in *War and Peace*, as we follow his attempts to realize himself and satisfy the spiritual yearnings he feels within him. He is constantly worrying "about life, about man's destiny." His inept, often clumsy character is echoed in his awkward spiritual quest, as he is by turns charitable and inconsequential, trying Freemasonry and even numerology in his attempt to find the truth for which he longs. Amidst all this Pierre is also capable of feeling deep emotions, falling in love, acting as a social mediator, offending people. This fullness of character enables him to take part in so much of the narrative, helping to hold its almost encyclopedic multifariousness together. And like Tolstoy himself, Pierre is capable of seeing into people, sometimes appearing to understand them better than they understand themselves, at other times hopelessly misjudging the social scene and showing himself up.

Typical is an encounter he has one evening with the retired general, "Old Bolkonsky," who is so pleased to see Pierre that he kisses him by way of welcoming him to his home. Together Pierre and the aged prince retire to his study before supper. Later Bolkonsky is heard

> hotly disputing with his visitor. Pierre was maintaining that a time would come when there were no more wars. The old prince disputed it chaffingly, but without getting angry.

"Drain the blood from men's veins and put in water instead, then there will be no more war! Old women's nonsense—old women's nonsense!" he repeated, but still patted Pierre affectionately on the shoulder.

Tolstoy intended that there should be something deeply sympathetic about Pierre, whose ingenuousness so matched that element in himself. At one point Pierre talks with Prince Andrei as they cross a river on a ferry. Pierre is attempting to persuade Andrei that there is a future life:

"You say you can't see a reign of goodness and truth on earth. Nor could I, and it cannot be seen if one looks on our life here as the end of everything. On *earth*, here on this earth" (Pierre pointed to the fields), "there is no truth, all is false and evil; but in the universe, in the whole universe, there is a kingdom of truth, and we who are now the children of earth are—eternally—children of the whole universe. Don't I feel in my soul that I am part of this vast harmonious whole?

Don't I feel that I form one link, one step, between the lower and higher beings in whom the Deity—the Supreme Power if you prefer the term—is manifest?"

But this is only a stage in Pierre's long journey of the soul—during his period of Freemasonry, as it happens. Later he is overcome by a malaise which brings him close to despair. Then he tries to lose himself in Moscow society:

Pierre no longer suffered moments of despair, hypochondria, and disgust with life, but the malady that had formerly found expression in such acute attacks was driven inwards and never left him for a moment. "What for? Why? What was going on in the world?" he would ask himself in perplexity.

But at this stage he couldn't help feeling that there were simply no answers to these questions, and he would hurry off to his club, to visit friends, to learn the latest gossip. At times he would try losing himself in reading. "He read, and read everything that came to hand. On coming home, while his valets were still taking off his things, he picked up a book and began to read." In his round of the drawing rooms and the club, exchanging and passing on gossip, he began drinking too much, even though his doctors warned him that this was bad for his corpulence. An aunt reprimanded him for his way of life, but soon drinking "became more and more a physical, almost a moral necessity." Yet even this was no use. "In the morning, on an empty stomach, all the old questions appeared as insoluble and terrible as ever."

Despite this, people enjoyed Pierre's company. There was something in his manner that enlivened the proceedings, whether at Masonic dinners, at the club, or in the salons. At the end of a jolly bachelor dinner, when others decided to set off on a jaunt, he would respond to their cheery invitations, joining them to shouts of delight from the company. Even so, he presented an odd figure: all were aware that he was different, a crank of sorts, especially the women whose company he so enjoyed:

At balls he danced if a partner was needed. Young ladies, married and unmarried, liked him because, without making love to any one of them, he was equally amiable to all, especially after supper. They said of him: "*Il est charmante. Il n'a pas de sexe.*" [He is charming. He has no sex.]

Early on in the book, after he has come into his inheritance, Pierre falls in love with the deceptively beautiful Hélène and they are married. Pierre proves to be the ideal husband for such a dazzling society woman as Hélène. His oddness, his occasional absentmindedness, his general social manner serve only to reinforce the brilliance of her salons, which soon assume almost legendary status. To be invited to one of these was regarded as the highest intellectual accolade: "Young men read books before attending Hélène's evenings, to have something to say in her salon, and secretaries of the embassy, and even ambassadors, confided diplomatic secrets to her, so that in a way Hélène was a power."

But Pierre is aware of her secret: he knows that she is in fact very stupid. Sometimes when he attends her salon he is overcome by a strange feeling of perplexity and fear amidst the discussions of politics, poetry, and philosophy. He feels like a conjurer who expects his trick to be unmasked at any moment, but this never happens, "perhaps because stupidity was just what was needed to run such a salon." So his wife's secret is never found out, and "her reputation as a lovely and clever woman became so firmly established that she could say the emptiest and stupidest things and yet everyone would go into raptures over every word of hers, and look for a profound meaning in it of which she herself had no conception." Inevitably Pierre's marriage would not be an easy one.

The central female figure of *War and Peace* is of course Natasha Rostov. In the second volume we see her attending her first ball, on New Year's Eve 1810. It is a very grand affair, with all the diplomatic corps and even the tsar himself in attendance at the grandee's mansion, on the English Quay in St. Petersburg. The mansion is glittering with lights amidst the winter night; dozens of police officers, led by the chief of police himself, stand on guard at the brightly lit entrance as the carriages arrive:

> From the carriages emerged men wearing uniforms, stars, and ribbons, while ladies in satin and ermine cautiously descended the carriage steps which were let down for them with a clatter, and then walked hurriedly and noiselessly over the baize at the entrance.

Natasha has been awake since eight in the morning in a fever of excitement. To the ball, she and her sister wear "white gauze over pink silk slips, with roses in their bodices, and their hair dressed *à la grecque.*" When Natasha first puts on her dress it turns out to be too long, and the maids must turn up the hem of her skirt. Upon her arrival, Natasha steps down from her carriage onto the red baize, enters the front hall, takes off her fur coat, and together with her mother and her sister mounts the brilliantly illuminated staircase between banks of flowers. "The mirrors on the landing reflected ladies in

white, pale blue, and pink dresses, with dia-
monds and pearls on their bare necks and arms."
Tolstoy manages to capture all the excitement
and wonder of Natasha, the mounting excitement before the entrance of the tsar, and eventually her dance with Prince Andrei.

> Prince Andrei was one of the best dancers of
> his day and Natasha danced exquisitely. Her
> little feet in their white satin dancing shoes
> did their work swiftly, lightly, and indepen-
> dent of herself, while her face beamed with
> ecstatic happiness.

Andrei finds himself comparing Natasha to
Hélène:

> Her slender bare arms and neck were not
> beautiful—compared to Hélène's her shoul-
> ders looked thin and her bosom undeveloped.
> But Hélène seemed, as it were, hardened by a
> varnish left by the thousands of looks that
> had scanned her person, while Natasha was
> like a girl exposed for the first time . . .
> scarcely had he embraced that slender supple

figure, and felt her stirring so close to him and smiling so near him, than the wine of her charm rose to his head.

By means of art that draws no attention to itself, Tolstoy assuredly conveys the scene with almost photographic clarity, at the same time making us aware of its nuances: the thoughts of Andrei, the different impressions made on him by Natasha and Hélène, the movement and closeness of the two swirling dancers, and Natasha's innocent excitement.

All this, and the other social scenes Tolstoy describes, are very much of their time and place—upper-class tsarist Russia in the first decade of the nineteenth century. Yet they are somehow timeless. Reading his words describing this scene of two hundred years ago we each experience in our own way what it must have been like. The very precision of his prose somehow forces us to imagine the scene; we feel we know what it was like, we are *there*. It is this power to provoke our imagination that makes Tolstoy so special when he evokes such scenes. What we see is like a film running before our mind, but this film evokes so much more than celluloid—we somehow *recognize* what is happening.

Yet this glittering social world eventually comes under threat. We join Pierre driving home in his sleigh through one icy winter night:

> It was clear and frosty. Above the dirty ill-lit streets, above the black roofs . . . at the entrance to Arbat Square an immense expanse of dark starry sky presented itself to his eyes. Almost in the center of it, above Prechistenka Boulevard, surrounded and sprinkled on all sides by stars but distinguished from them all by its nearness to the earth, its white light, and its long uplifted tail, shone the enormous and brilliant comet of the year 1812—the comet which was said to portend all kinds of woes and the end of the world.

Pierre himself is not frightened by this omen; he is in love, for the moment unconcerned by the great events about to unfold around him. In the summer of 1812 Napoleon and his Grand Army invaded Russia; and thus, in Tolstoy's words, "an event took place opposed to human reason and to human nature." Tolstoy cannot disguise his disgust and anger at this betrayal of humanity and what it caused:

> Millions of men perpetrated against one another such innumerable crimes, frauds, treacheries, thefts, forgeries, issues of false money, burglaries, incendiarisms, and murders, as in whole centuries are not recorded in the annals of all the law courts of the world, but which those who committed them did not at the time regard as being crimes.

With this telling image Tolstoy suggests a whole world turned upside down, with humanity bereft of all sense and morality. He now asks, "What produced this extraordinary occurrence? What were the causes?" He examines the many reasons put forward by historians at the time, also the actions of Napoleon and Tsar Alexander I. But in the end he seems to suggest that the huge interlocking forces by which every individual is linked with others to form the world in which they live, all these contribute. We each, in our own way, help produce the "fatalism" of such events, and Tolstoy sees the main ingredient of this concept as "fate" rather than our more usual reading of "resignation":

> We are forced to fall back on fatalism as an explanation of irrational events (that is to say, the reasonableness of which we do not understand). The more we try to explain such events in history reasonably, the more unreasonable and incomprehensible do they become to us.
>
> Each man lives for himself, using his freedom to attain his personal aims, and feels with his whole being that he can now do or abstain from doing this or that action; but as soon as he has done it, that action performed at a certain moment in time becomes irrevocable and belongs to history, in which it has not a free but a predestined significance.

What he appears to be arguing here is that all our individual free wills contribute to a collective determinism. The precise mechanics by which this free will becomes determinism remains un-

70

clear. If it becomes determinism because it has entered the past (and thus cannot be changed), this is obvious. By the same count, the determinism of the past certainly affects our present, but it does not render it determined, because in the present we have free will. Tolstoy's point here seems to be either trivial or plain wrong.

The same certainly cannot be said of the last two volumes of *War and Peace,* which contain many of the finest and most stirring scenes in Western literature. In his magnificent descriptions of the battle of Borodino, the taking of Moscow, and Napoleon's retreat from Moscow, Tolstoy evokes the great events that took place. With soldiers looting, the shooting of prisoners, the lynchings and the mob on the rampage, Tolstoy depicts the horrors of war. With Napoleon, Tsar Alexander I, and Marshal Kutuzov, he depicts its leading figures. But most impressive is how the roles of his individual characters run like a thread through these events, as the likes of Pierre, Prince Andrei, and Natasha play their parts, their individual destinies unraveling amidst the movements of greater historical events. Here, afloat on what Tolstoy describes as "the sea of history," is the ship we all sail in. We all think we guide it in our own separate ways when the sea is calm, but "as soon as a storm arises and the sea begins to heave and the ship to move, such a delusion is no longer possible."

As one would expect with such an overwhelming masterpiece, the eventual publication of *War and Peace* was met with widespread acclaim. Even so, many critics could not resist pointing out its flaws—the largely aristocratic viewpoint, the intrusive philosophizing, as well as its vast, sometimes unwieldy length, which on occasions led to confusion or tedium. Yet none could deny the sheer power of much of its writing. Nonetheless the criticisms would become a cause for complaint when the first English and French translations began appearing. In the view of these foreign critics more used to the "art" of the novel, Tolstoy appeared undisciplined, a force of nature not properly absorbed into the form of art. (This had been how the aesthetically sophisticated French critics had for many years viewed Shakespeare.) Tolstoy would gradually emerge as a name to rank alongside that of Shakespeare, Dante, and Goethe. And perhaps it is no coincidence that both Dante and Goethe have been accused of attempting to use their works as a vehicle for their ideas. Any writer attempting such an all-inclusive vision of the world and history is surely bound to include within that vision his idea of how the world works, and the philosophy with which he views it. Modern critics are beginning to realize that even Shakespeare's vision was slightly more didactic than has previously been supposed—with his "objective" historical plays being filled with covert messages about the Elizabethan world in which they appeared, with many subtle meanings that have now become lost to us. As Tolstoy seems to illustrate, it is very difficult for a great vision to be other than some sort of moral vision too.

Now forty-one years old, with the success of *War and Peace* Tolstoy no longer had money problems. His financial security was largely due to the influence of his wife Sofia, who quickly recognized Tolstoy's incompetence where money was concerned and took over as his business manager. It was she who sensed that *War and Peace* would make much more money in book form than if it were published in installments in magazines, and she prevented him from selling the copyright of his great work for a pittance.

Tolstoy now began reading philosophy, devoting himself mostly to the works of the melancholic German philosopher Schopenhauer, whose pessimistic writings had recently become the rage in Germany. (Tolstoy's great musical contemporary, Richard Wagner, would also be similarly struck by Schopenhauer around this time.) According to Schopenhauer, the world and all within it are determined by an evil will, and mankind's only hope is to negate his own ego, thus suppressing the part of this evil will that runs through him. For such a gargantuan ego as Tolstoy, this indeed presented a challenge; resignation was completely contrary to his nature. Even so, he would make the attempt. Almost certainly as a result of this misguided spiritual exercise, he had a frightening spiritual experience, of which he wrote: "I was overcome by despair, fear and terror, the like of which I have never experienced before." The fatalism that had permeated the last volumes of *War and Peace* in the form of "fate" now began to assume its more passive, depressive, despairing features in his life. But at heart Tolstoy was no fatalist: he could not resign himself to utter despair. He resisted the bleakness that now so overwhelmed him by placing himself in the hands of God. Around this time he declared, "I believe in God, in the expression in the Gospel that not one hair falls unless willed by the Lord. Therefore I say that all is predestined."

Most people who fall into such a depressive state are overcome by sloth. But not Tolstoy. In 1870 he embarked upon another huge novel about Peter the Great, the tsar who in the early years of the previous century had founded modern Russia, built St. Petersburg, and attempted to introduce European ways into his backward empire. Tolstoy would work at this novel for four years before finally abandoning it, eventually admitting that the subject had overwhelmed him and was totally unsuited to his talents.

A year later he embarked upon what he described as his first "real novel" (that is, its purpose would not be didactic). This work would be published in regular installments in the magazine *Russian Herald* as he wrote it, but would not be completed until three years later in 1877. The result was *Anna Karenina*, Tolstoy's second great masterpiece.

In many ways *Anna Karenina* has a far more coherent artistic structure than *War and Peace*. But although it may be artistically superior and without the flaws that mar that earlier work, it never quite rises to such transcendent heights. That said, there is no denying the huge merits of *Anna Karenina*, which is prefaced with the forbidding epitaph "Vengeance is mine; I will repay," and its tragic climax is indeed a fitting example of God's wrath. The work opens with perhaps the most famous first line in the history of the novel: "All happy families are alike, each unhappy family is unhappy in its own way."

Anna Karenina does indeed deal with family life and is set in the upper-class Russian society of the 1860s, a period which Tolstoy had experienced firsthand around the time of his own marriage. In keeping with his philosophical reading, this novel has an underlying pessimism that was not present in *War and Peace*, despite all its so-called "fatalism." Central to the vast unwinding plot of *Anna Karenina*, which devolves in so many strands of social life, is the adulterous affair between Anna and Count Vronsky. This sinful love is contrasted with the righteous love of Kitty and Levin, who end up creating a marriage rather than destroying one. Their happy liaison was inspired by Tolstoy's own marriage, yet at the same time it is all too easy to recognize Tolstoy's own agonizing in that of Levin, with his thoughts about suicide, the meaning of life, and what could be done to allieviate the lot of the peasantry.

The paragraph immediately after the opening generalization plunges the reader directly into a particular situation:

Everything was upset in the Oblonskys' house. The wife had discovered an intrigue between her husband and their former French governess, and declared that she would not continue to live under the same roof with him. This state of things had now lasted for three days, and not only the husband and wife but the rest of the family and the whole of the household suffered from it. They all felt that there was no sense in their living together, and that any group of people who had met together by chance at an inn would have had more in common than they.

This moves neatly from the particular to the wider psychological effect. The one unhappy revelation had destroyed not only a relationship and a family but also an entire household, now in a state of upheaval. As Tolstoy goes on to record, the wife stayed in her part of the house, the husband stayed away all day, even the children were upset, playing their games and running about the house as usual, but "uneasily." The ripples of effect fan outward. The English governess has quarreled with the housekeeper, making the governess so upset that she has written to her friend asking if she knows of another post. The cook had simply left the house at dinnertime the previous day and not returned, so there were no meals. Meanwhile the kitchen maid and the coachman had handed in their notices. The central lynchpin of the family had been withdrawn, and the entire social edifice had begun to fall apart.

A few days later the husband, Prince Steven Oblonsky, awakes on the morocco sofa in his study. He lies in the dark remembering his dream. Then suddenly he comes to, realizing where he is, realizing why he is sleeping on his sofa and not in bed beside his wife, as he has done for the past nine years. The nightmare becomes personal, and he remembers what has happened: "the details of his quarrel with his wife, his inextricable position, and, worst of all, his guilt rose up in his imagination."

The Oblonskys introduce the theme of adulterous betrayal, which will be played out in the intense but fated love affair of Anna and Vronsky. Tolstoy explores the emotions and evasions, the strengths and indulgences of his central characters. Because he is dealing with their feelings, he understands the need to probe deeply into their psychology. Yet Anna and Vronsky are never less than alive to us. Tolstoy allows us to see them at the same time as he allows us to see through them. We cannot help but be involved, yet recoil at the same time we sympathize with them, as they celebrate and endure all the pangs of love. Their early meetings and guilty uncertainties are beautifully suggested, forcing us imaginatively to reconstruct in our minds these scenes which we feel are so real that the author must surely be remembering incidents from his own life.

> She wore a white dress trimmed with wide embroidery, and as she sat in a corner of the veranda behind some plants, did not hear Vronsky coming. Bowing her curly head she pressed her forehead against a cold watering-can that stood on the balustrade, and both her beautiful hands, with the rings he knew so well, were holding the can. The beauty of her whole figure, her head, her neck, and her arms, always struck Vronsky with new surprise. He stopped, gazing at her with rapture.

But just as he was going to step toward her, she felt his nearness, pushed away the can, and turned her hot face toward him.

Slowly and inexorably the tale unfolds against the background of a brilliant, privileged, and hypocritical society, slowly and inexorably it moves toward its fateful climax. This is a love story, but it is also a tragedy.

While nearing the end of writing *Anna Karenina*, Tolstoy found himself entering a state of ever-increasing spiritual crisis. Fortunately this did not seem to affect his writing. Yet the crisis did not end when he finished the book, and by 1879, more than a year after *Anna Karenina* had been published to great acclaim, he was on the point of suicide.

Despite his happy marriage, his fame throughout Russia, and his burgeoning wealth, his ever-persistent self-questioning had led him to the point of no return. In a valiant effort to rouse himself, he began visiting monasteries, seeking advice from several well-known wise priests. But more and more he found himself questioning even their faith, along with his belief in the Orthodoxy of the Russian church. He still fervently believed in God, but not in the way they worshiped Him. Only the peasants seemed to have the answer. In living as they did, they served God, not themselves. The lesson seemed evident: the true life was lived for God, not for oneself. In 1879 Tolstoy wrote *A Confession*, which traced the vicissitudes of his spiritual life, much in the manner of St. Augustine's *Confessions*. The book emphasized his increasing alienation from the Russian Orthodox church, pointing out how it was

> quite impossible to judge by a man's life and conduct whether he is a believer or not. If there is a difference between a man who publicly professes Orthodoxy and one who denies it, the difference is not in favor of the former . . . the public profession and confession of Orthodoxy were chiefly met with among people who were dull and cruel and who considered themselves very important. Ability, honesty, reliability, good-nature, and

moral conduct were more often met with among unbelievers.

Only the Orthodoxy of the peasants was condoned, and even this hardly shed a good light on the church: "How often I envied the peasants their illiteracy and lack of learning! Those statements in the creed which to me were evident absurdities for them contained nothing false." Not surprisingly, *A Confession* was banned by the authorities: God, the tsar, and the Holy Church were intricately bound together; they were the preservation of Russia. Tolstoy's writings were viewed as seditious, almost revolutionary. Had he not been a revered writer and a member of one of the leading families in the land, he would certainly have been flung into prison.

Tolstoy now underwent a conversion of sorts, which led him to believe in the teachings of the New Testament: only living in the manner of Christ could give life meaning. This belief soon took on its own unique Tolstoyan form. The scattered insights and questionings that had appeared in both his novels and his diaries coalesced into a credo. He believed that each and every person had within him a power to distinguish between good and evil. When they attuned themselves to this power it informed their ability to reason properly as well as providing them with a conscience. To follow the promptings of this power gave meaning to people's lives, enabling them to do good. This belief led Tolstoy to set down five commandments, which he claimed were Christ's true teaching (as distinct from the distorted version that had been handed down by the church). These five commandments were: do not get angry, do not give way to lust, do not bind yourself with oaths, do not resist a person who is evil, be good to both the just and the unjust.

Tolstoy's beliefs now led him to become a Christian anarchist pacifist, and his writings took on a completely different tenor, as can be seen from the titles of some of the works he produced during this period: *What I Believe, What Must We Do?, The Kingdom of God Is Within You.* They more resembled dogmatic pamphlets than literature, though *What Must We Do?* contains a powerful description of his visits to the Moscow slums and the squalor he found there. It also addresses the very real problem of poverty in Russia, unmasking how much of the population still lived in a state of virtual slavery. As usual with Tolstoy's work of this period, it also traces a spiritual journey: "Only when I began to look on myself as a man like all others, did my path become plain to me." It ends with a tirade against property and some distinctly backward views on the place of women in society: "Women's real work is to bear children. . . . Within memory, woman's fall—her dereliction of her duty—has begun, and within my memory it has spread more and more widely."

Yet Tolstoy was still capable of powerful writing, despite his overwhelming beliefs. Evidence of this is to be seen in his 1889 story "The Kreutzer Sonata," a compelling work despite the many ludicrous ideas expressed in it. Chief among these is Tolstoy's prohibitive view of sex, which he had now come to regard as no more than an evil animal lust, no matter in what form it appeared. Thus marriage was nothing but a low sham. At one point in the story Tolstoy mentions a Parisian sideshow with a bearded woman and a "water-dog." The character Pozdnyshev tells how he paid and went into the booth, only to discover that the bearded woman was simply a man in woman's clothing and the so-called water-dog was just a dog wrapped in a walrus skin swimming in a bath. When Pozdnyshev leaves, the booth owner tells the waiting public to ask the gentleman whether or not it is a good show. Pozdnyshev is too ashamed of himself to reveal the truth and tell the others that the whole thing is a sham. This is just what marriage is like, he explains to his listener. This is but a small incident in "The Kreutzer Sonata," but it is characteristic of its author's attitude throughout.

In 1895 the sixty-seven-year-old Tolstoy embarked upon another novel, with the ominously religious title *Resurrection*. It took him four years to complete and contained flashes of his old genius, particularly in its famous court scene, but for the most part the novel is ruined by the author's intrusive moralizing. The book is prefaced with a bevy of biblical epigraphs, including,

"He that is without sin among you, let him first cast a stone at her." Briefly, the plot tells of a young girl, Maslova, who has been seduced by a nobleman, Nekhlyudov. She becomes a prostitute, is falsely accused of a crime, and is sent to Siberia. Nekhlyudov, who coincidentally serves on the trial jury, is overcome by conscience and follows her to Siberia with the intention of marrying her. *Resurrection* is meant to illustrate the overwhelming power of love as well as to depict the injustices and corruption so prevalent in the Russian system. Nekhlyudov's eventual conversion to Christ-like ideas of forgiveness and spiritual love is all too predictable.

By now Tolstoy was giving away much of his earnings from writing to famine relief, the support of a Christian sect that had emigrated to Canada, and similar worthy causes. His wife and family were becoming increasingly disenchanted, not sharing his wish to live in Christ-like poverty. Even the peasants on his estate grew disgruntled with their master's wish to live as they did yet reside in his large country house. They too had no wish to continue living in "holy poverty."

Tolstoy's ideas had now begun to attract a number of "thinkers" who traveled as disciples to Yasnaya Polyana, where they would be shown around the estate by their bearded, smock-clad host so that they could see for themselves the benefits of the Christ-like life.

In order to clarify his ideas on the relevance of literature and the arts to his Christ-like beliefs, Tolstoy now embarked upon a work called "What Is Art?" By this time he believed that art should employ simple forms to express moral truths. This led him into a series of earnest arguments enlivened only by flashes of absurdity. At one point he tells a simple children's story about a chicken stealing some wheat flour, and claims that such art is better than Zola, Huysmans, and other fine French authors of the time. Turning to Shakespeare, he rules out *Hamlet* for being only one of those "false imitations of works of art." Instead he prefers a theatrical performance put on "in a small tent-house" by a savage tribe called the Voguls, during which "the audience . . . are paralyzed with suspense; deep groans and even weeping are heard among them." Although he admits that he never actually saw this performance, but only read about it, "from the mere description I felt that this was a true work of art." Beethoven's Ninth Symphony is similarly rubbished. Only "art which is infected by the author's condition of soul" is worth anything at all. Soulless Beethoven, false Shakespeare, and adult Zola are all dimissed. This might be simply ridiculous if it were not for the chilling fact that Tolstoy's prescription for art bears an uncanny resemblance to the socialist realism and quaint moral folktales that would become compulsory fare during the Communist era in Russia, whose dawn was just two decades away. How fortunate we are that *War and Peace* and *Anna Karenina* were written before Tolstoy knew what he was doing.

By 1901 the Orthodox church had had enough of Tolstoy, and he was solemnly excommunicated—no small matter in Russia at this time. Two years later, by now an obstinate seventy-six-year-old, Tolstoy swore that he would publish no further creative works. This was more a matter of stubbornness than Tolstoyan principle—Sofia was doing her best to keep much-needed income flowing into Yasnaya Polyana to feed the large family, which now included twelve children, and Tolstoy resented how well she was managing his business affairs.

By this time Tolstoy's strictures against the lusts of the flesh had long since put an end to intimate relations with Sofia. He had also given up alcohol and tobacco as well as becoming a vegetarian. In his quest for self-sufficiency he insisted upon cobbling his own boots, which he wore with his peasant smock.

Yasnaya Polyana became a great attraction for converts to Tolstoy's religion, and many disciples made protracted stays, supporting the master in his quarrels with his wife and family. By 1905 Sofia was driven to such distraction that she was threatening suicide.

But Tolstoy was indefatigable. He was now on his way to turning his religion into a world religion. He began assembling a large work consisting of passages from the saints, wise men, and shamans of all religions, with the aim of demonstrating that all religions were in fact the same, that their fundamental beliefs were no different from his own. The only reason they appeared to be different from one another was because the priests and later interpreters of these religions had corrupted the truth preached by their original founders. It appeared that the crucified Christ, the potbellied beatific Buddha, and the warrior Muhammad were all really the same at heart.

The anomalies of Tolstoy's own existence were now becoming unbearable to him. How could he preach that we should live a life of Christ-like self-sufficiency, encumbered with as few possessions as possible, when he himself was burdened with an extensive estate, all his serfs, and his large family—at least one member of which had now become intolerable to him. Sofia felt much the same; life at Yasnaya Polyana was becoming impossible for both of them. Tolstoy still kept his intimate diary, which inevitably contained many hurtful observations about Sofia. Yet as before he insisted there be no secrets between them, and that she should read what he had written. She too now kept an intimate diary, which he read. Both poured out their thoughts about their marriage, and in the process denigrated each other—at the same time aware that the other would read their words. This psychological intimacy bound them together at the same time they were tearing each other apart. Such an impossible situation had already driven Sofia to the brink of suicide and contributed greatly to Tolstoy's self-image of religious martyrdom. On top of this were continuing quarrels between Tolstoy and his wife over the copyright of his works, which Sofia insisted upon retaining in order to provide for the family's future.

In the end Tolstoy decided he had endured more than he could bear. Now aged eighty-two, he hatched a secret plot to escape. He would take to the road, become a pilgrim, and live a Christ-like life unburdened by trivial worries and possessions. On October 28, 1910, the aged Tolstoy left Yasnaya Polyana with just a few possessions and a walking stick, setting off into the chill air of the Russian night. The pilgrim was in fact accompanied by his personal physician and trunks packed by his daughter, and driven from his estate in a carriage to the nearest railway station. The next train was not due for an hour, and Tolstoy fretted, terrified that his wife would discover he had departed and come after him. But the train arrived, and he was soon on his way. When Sofia discovered what had happened, she ran from the house and threw herself into the pond—but landed in shallow water and was rescued by the servants before she could make a more convincing attempt to drown herself.

Some hours later news of what had happened reached Moscow, and soon the newspapers were appearing with headlines: "Tolstoy Vanishes from Yasnaya Polyana!"

A few days later Tolstoy had made it as far as Astopova, where he fell ill at the railway station. A bed was made for him in the station waiting room, and the ailing pilgrim was quickly recognized. In no time, family, disciples, and reporters were rushing to the scene to pay homage to the Christ-like figure recumbent in his bed. Sofia arrived, but disciples prevented her from disturbing the saint in the waiting room; as she paced up and down the platform in a hysterical state, foreign journalists and newsreel reporters poured from the incoming trains. It was plain that Tolstoy had not long to live. On November 7 the bearded figure in the station waiting room at Astopova finally succumbed to pneumonia. The news was telegraphed around the world.

Afterword

As Tolstoy's work was translated into the major European languages and then beyond, he became recognized as the greatest writer of his age. But what precisely had he written? It was so difficult to place many of Tolstoy's works. Initially *War and Peace*, and even *Anna Karenina,* were not regarded as novels in the usually accepted Western tradition. According to the critics, they included too many "ideas," too much intrusion of the author's voice, to be viewed purely as works of literature. Nonetheless they were soon acknowledged by readers as a supreme production of the human spirit—it hardly mattered what category they fitted into. The effect of *War and Peace* and

Anna Karenina is perhaps best summed up by the British critic John Bayley, who declared, "The pair seem not so much novels as wise and dense areas of experience which insensibly become a part of our own." So vivid and involving are these works that it is as if they enter our lives.

Curiously, it was at first Tolstoy's ideas that had the greatest impact—and they did this through their influence upon a few exceptional human beings. The inspirational Indian leader Mahatma Gandhi was deeply affected by Tolstoy's idealistic writings, calling him "The most truthful man of his age." Gandhi was especially influenced by Tolstoy's views on pacifism and nonviolence. When Gandhi led the struggle for Indian independence from British rule, the principle of nonviolent action would be his main weapon, the means by which the powerless Indian people learned to resist their powerful colonial governors. Later these same Tolstoyan principles would be used in sit-ins by antinuclear demonstrators and the American civil rights movement.

Another leading twentieth-century figure to be deeply influenced by Tolstoy's ideas was the Austrian philosopher Ludwig Wittgenstein. During a low period while serving with the Austro-Hungarian army in World War I, Wittgenstein came across a ransacked bookshop in Galicia which contained just one book: Tolstoy's commentary on the Gospels. Its effect would transform the way Wittgenstein lived his life. Already uncomfortable with his inherited wealth, he now resolved to give away his entire fortune. Tolstoy's ideas had a similar effect upon his philosophy: what for Wittgenstein had previously been an intellectual matter now became infused with moral purpose.

Tolstoy's works would also have a profound negative effect, if unintentionally so. When Lenin read Tolstoy's ideas, he immediately saw the threat to his own Communist principles. Tolstoy's ideas might be far more appealing to the Russian people than the Germanic idea of communism which he planned to introduce into Russia. With this in mind, Lenin wrote, "Tolstoyism should be fought all along the line." Naturally, Stalin would take an equally negative view of Tolstoy. But when Germany invaded Russia during the early years of World War II, Stalin took the Machiavellian decision to use the patriotism of Tolstoy's works to inspire the Russians to resist the Nazis. One hundred fifty thousand copies of *Sebastopol Sketches* were rushed from the official printers and distributed to the people, and patriotic passages from *War and Peace* were posted in the streets of Moscow. Soon there were more of Tolstoy's works in print than there were of Lenin's—though this situation would not outlast the war. Nowadays the works of Lenin are all but ignored in Russia while the works of Tolstoy have been returned to their rightful place at the pinnacle of literature, both in Russia and throughout the world.

From Tolstoy's Writings

From the early short story "The Raid":

Our troops had taken possession of the village and not a single soul of the enemy remained in it. . . . The long clean huts, with their flat earthen roofs and shapely chimneys, stood on irregular stoney mounds between which flowed a small stream. . . . A moment later, dragoons, Cossacks, and infantry spread with evident delight through the crooked lanes and in an instant the empty village was animated again. . . . Here is a Cossack dragging along a sack of flour and a carpet, there a soldier, with a delighted look on his face, brings a tin basin and some rag out of a hut, another is trying with outstretched arms to catch two hens that struggle and cackle beside a fence, a third has somewhere discovered an enormous pot of milk and after drinking some of it throws the rest on the ground with a loud laugh.

An operating room at the siege of Sebastopol, from the first of Tolstoy's Sebastopol Sketches:

There you will see doctors with pale, gloomy faces, and arms red with blood up to the elbows, busy at a bed on which a wounded man lies under chloroform. His eyes are open and he utters, as if in delirium, incoherent but sometimes simple and pathetic words. The doctors are engaged upon the horrible but beneficent work of amputation. You will see the sharp curved knife enter the healthy white flesh; you will see the wounded man come back to life with terrible, heart-rending screams and curses. You will see the doctor's assistant toss the amputated arm into a corner, and in the same room you will see another wounded man on a stretcher watching the operation, and writhing and groaning not so much from physical pain as from the mental torture of anticipation.

Olenin approaches Maryanka, the Cossack girl with whom he has fallen in love, from The Cossacks:

She suddenly turned. There was a scarcely perceptible trace of tears in her eyes and her face was beautiful in its sadness. . . .

"What are you crying for? What is it?"

"What?" she repeated in a rough voice. "Cossacks have been killed. That's what for. . . . Go away! What do you want?"

"Maryanka!" said Olenin, approaching her.

"You will never get anything from me!"

"Maryanka, don't speak like that," Olenin entreated.

"Get away. I'm sick of you!" shouted the girl, stamping her foot, and moving threateningly toward him. And her face expressed such abhorrence, such contempt, and such anger that Olenin suddenly understood that there was no hope for him, and that his first impression of this woman's inaccessibility had been perfectly correct.

Olenin said nothing more, but ran out of the hut.

Early in Anna Karenina *Levin encounters Vronsky, his rival for the hand of Kitty:*

There are people who when they meet a rival, no matter in what, at once shut their eyes to everything good in him and see only the bad. There are others who on the contrary try to discern in a lucky rival the qualities which have enabled him to succeed, and with aching hearts seek only the good in him. Levin belonged to the latter sort. But it was not difficult for him to see what was good and attractive in Vronsky. It struck him immediately. Vronsky was a dark sturdily built man of medium height, with a good-natured, handsome, exceedingly quiet and firm face. Everything about his face and figure—from his black closely cropped hair and freshly shaven chin to his wide, brand-new uniform—was simple and at the same time elegant. . . . Having greeted and spoken a few words to everyone else, he sat down without having looked once at Levin, who had not taken his eyes off him.

Anna Karenina's tragic end:

But she did not take her eyes off the wheels of the approaching second truck, and at the very moment when the midway point between the wheels drew level, she threw away her red bag, and drawing her head down between her shoulders threw herself forward on her hands under the truck, and with a light movement, as if preparing to rise again, immediately dropped on her knees. At the same moment she was horror-struck at what she was doing. "Where am I? What am I doing? Why?" She wished to rise, to throw herself back, but something huge and relentless struck her on the head and dragged her down. "God forgive me everything!" she said, feeling the impossibility of struggling. . . .

From "I Cannot Be Silent," Tolstoy's polemic against the death penalty, commenting on twelve executions reported in the newspaper:

Twelve husbands, fathers, and sons, from among those whose kindness, industry, and simplicity alone rests the whole of Russian life, are seized, imprisoned, and shackled. Then their hands are tied behind their backs lest they should seize the ropes by which they are to be hung, and they are led to the gallows. Several peasants similar to those about to be hung, but armed, dressed in clean soldiers' uniforms with good boots on their feet and guns in their hands, accompany the condemned men. Beside them walks a long-haired man, wearing a stole and vestments of gold or silver cloth and bearing a cross.

From "What Is Art?":

How is one to discriminate? . . . For a country peasant of unperverted taste this is as easy as it is for an animal of unspoilt scent to follow the trace he needs among a thousand others in wood or forest. The animal unerringly finds what he needs. So also the man, if only his natural qualities have not been perverted, will without fail select from among thousands of objects the real work of art he requires—that which infects him with the feeling experienced by the artist. But it is not so with those whose taste has been perverted by their education and life. The receptive feeling of these people is atrophied, and in valuing artistic productions they must be guided by discussion and study, which discussion and study completely confuse them. So that most people in our society are quite unable to distinguish a work of art from the grossest counterfeits.

Tolstoy's Chief Works in English Translation

Childhood[†]
Sebastopol Sketches[†]
Early Short Stories[†]
The Cossacks[*][†]
War and Peace[*][†]
Anna Karenina[*][†]
A Confession[†]
The Kreutzer Sonata[*][†]
How Much Land Does a Man Need?
Resurrection[*][†]

[*]major works
[†]discussed in text

Master and Man
Hadji Murad
What Is Art?[†]
I Cannot Be Silent

Chronology of
Tolstoy's Life and Times

1828   August 28 old-style calendar (September 9 new calendar), birth of Leo Nikolaevich Tolstoy at Yasnaya Polyana in the province of Tula, the fourth son of Count Nikolaevich Ilyich Tolstoy.

1830   Tolstoy's mother dies.

1837   Family settles in Moscow. Death of Tolstoy's father.

1838   Publication of Dickens's *Oliver Twist*.

1844   Tolstoy enters Kazan University.

1851   Tolstoy travels to Caucasus to join brother Nikolai. Opening of St.

Petersburg-to-Moscow railway, the first in Russia. Publication of *Communist Manifesto* by Marx and Engels.

1852   Tolstoy enters army. *Childhood* published.

1853   Outbreak of Crimean War, with Russia confronted by French and British armies.

1854   Tolstoy at siege of Sebastopol.

1855   Death of Tsar Nicholas I and accession of Alexander II.

1856   End of Crimean War.

1857   Tolstoy travels to Western Europe, visiting Paris, Switzerland, and Germany.

1859   Publication of Darwin's *Origin of Species*.

1861   Tsar Alexander II emancipates the serfs. Tolstoy travels to Europe to consult German educators. Outbreak of American Civil War.

1862   Marries Sofia Behrs, daughter of a court physician.

1863   Son Sergei born.

1863–1869	Writing *War and Peace.*
1866	Publication of Dostoevsky's *Crime and Punishment.*
1870	Franco-Prussian War ends in French defeat. Paris Commune. Birth of Lenin.
1873–1877	Writing *Anna Karenina.*
1879	Writes *A Confession.*
1880	Birth of Stalin.
1882	Assassination of Tsar Alexander II. Death of Dostoevsky.
1889	Tolstoy publishes *The Kreutzer Sonata.*
1891	Work begins on Trans-Siberian Railway.
1895–1899	Writing *Resurrection.*
1898	Writes *What Is Art?*
1901	Tolstoy excommunicated from Russian Orthodox church.
1904	Outbreak of Russo-Japanese War.

1905   Widespread unrest in Russia; mutiny on battleship *Potemkin*.

1910   October: Tolstoy flees Yasnaya Polyana. Dies of pneumonia on November 7 old-style calendar (November 20 new calendar) at Astopova station at age of eighty-two.

Recommended Reading

John Bayley, ed., *The Portable Tolstoy* (Penguin Books, 1978). A wide-ranging selection of the master's work, including many of his finest stories and essays, ranging from the early *Childhood* to the late *A Confession*. This is ideal as a sampler, which can be read before starting into the great two novels, which are not included. The selection was edited by the husband of the novelist Iris Murdoch, and he provides a brief insightful introduction.

Donna Tussing Orwin, ed., *The Cambridge Companion to Tolstoy* (Cambridge University Press, 2002). One of the latest additions to this highly acclaimed series, it includes informative and readable essays by experts on many aspects of

Tolstoy's life and works. The position of women and the family in Tolstoy are discussed by Edwina Cruise, professor of Russian at Mount Holyoke College. The collection also includes a forty-five-page chronology of Tolstoy's life and works, which can be read as a useful short biography.

George Steiner, *Tolstoy or Dostoevsky: An Essay in the Old Criticism* (Yale University Press, 1996). This 350-page "essay" by the great modern critic contrasts the two Russian giants of the nineteenth century. As Steiner himself points out in his preface, "This is a young man's book. It was written, as first books ought to be, out of sheer compulsion." *The Times* of London called Steiner's book "criticism in the grand manner," an appraisal that is true of all Steiner's work. As ever, Steiner likes to give the impression that he knows absolutely everything about his subject—and this makes his book a joy to read for any aficionado of Tolstoy's work.

Leo Tolstoy, *War and Peace*, trans. by Louise and Aylmer Maude (Oxford University Press, 1998). Tolstoy's masterpiece and regarded by many as the greatest novel ever written. This translation is by the Maudes, who knew Russia well and were friends of Tolstoy himself. Tolstoy, who knew some English, was highly impressed by the Maudes' translation and expressed his deep gratitude. The work is almost fifteen hundred pages, and its vast sweep carries the reader from 1805 through the historic and horrific events of 1812 when Napoleon invaded Russia, and beyond. Some of its scenes of Russian social life and the great battles (particularly Borodino) have never been equaled. The main characters, especially Pierre and Natasha, are similarly memorable.

Leo Tolstoy, *Anna Karenina*, trans. by Louise and Aylmer Maude (Dover Publications, 2004). This is Tolstoy's second masterpiece and deals with social events closer to his own time. Its central theme is based on a real-life scandal that rocked Russian society in the 1860s. The central figure of Anna is one of the great tragic love heroines of all literature. The book contains many memorable scenes of glittering Russian high society but also reveals the moral malaise at the heart of that society. This too is a lengthy work, extending to almost a thousand pages in most editions. The Maudes' translation is recommended and was praised by Tolstoy himself.

Henri Troyat, *Tolstoy* (Grove Press, 2001). This work by the celebrated French Academician remains the best-known biography of Tolstoy. Its seven hundred pages are filled with dramatic detail, and it is never less than interesting, even if it sometimes extends itself beyond the known facts. The translation by Nancy Amphoux reads faultlessly and captures all the flair of the original French. It also contains many fascinating photos of Tolstoy and his family.

A. N. Wilson, *Tolstoy: A Biography* (W. W. Norton, 2001). This more modern biography by a well-known contemporary British novelist and commentator unfolds with all the verve of a skilled wordsmith intent upon telling, in his own way, the fascinating story of Tolstoy's life. Wilson's talent is particularly suited to the investigation of Tolstoy's religious, spiritual, and moral preoccupations. His meticulous research also succeeds in bringing the Russian background to life.

Index

A NOTE ON THE AUTHOR

Paul Strathern has lectured in philosophy and mathematics and now lives and writes in London. He is the author of the enormously successful series Philosophers in 90 Minutes. A Somerset Maugham Prize winner, he is also the author of books on history and travel, as well as five novels. His articles have appeared in a great many publications, including the *Observer* (London) and the *Irish Times*.

Paul Strathern's 90 Minutes series in philosophy, also published by Ivan R. Dee, includes individual books on Thomas Aquinas, Aristotle, St. Augustine, Berkeley, Confucius, Derrida, Descartes, Dewey, Foucault, Hegel, Heidegger, Hume, Kant, Kierkegaard, Leibniz, Locke, Machiavelli, Marx, J. S. Mill, Nietzsche, Plato, Rousseau, Bertrand Russell, Sartre, Schopenhauer, Socrates, Spinoza, and Wittgenstein.

NOW PUBLISHED IN THIS SERIES:

IN PREPARATION: